The Truth of Two

Selected Translations

Harry Thomas

The Truth of Two

Selected Translations

Harry Thomas

2017
Un-Gyve Press
Boston

Designed by Un-Gyve Limited

Manufactured in the United States of America

FIRST EDITION

10 9 8 7 6 5 4 3 2 1

Library of Congress Control Number:
2017955311

ISBN: 978-0-9993632-2-5

Contents

Acknowledgements

I wish to express my gratitude to the editors of the journals in which these translations first appeared: *Agni*, *American Poetry Review*, *Berfrois*, *Cauldron*, *Crisis*, *The Formalist*, *Harvard Review*, *Hobart Park*, *Literary Imagination*, *Los Angeles Review*, *Metre*, *Michigan Quarterly Review*, *Modern Poetry in Translation*, *Partisan Review*, *Poetry Daily*, *PN*, *Poetry Northwest*, *Practices of the Wind*, *Salamander*, *Times Literary Supplement*, *Two Lines*, *Threepenny Review*, and *TriQuarterly*.

My lasting gratitude also goes to friends who read drafts of translations and helped to improve them: Lee Gerlach, Larry Goldstein, and Margarita Pazmany. I feel a bottomless debt to David Ferry and Christopher Ricks. The days I spent with Joseph Brodsky—in Ann Arbor, San Diego, New York, Boston, and Baja—remain a great joy. I dedicate this book to his memory.

For this book and for *Some Complicity* two years ago, to Julie and Lisa Nemrow, creators and editors of Un-Gyve, my admiration and special thanks.

Preface

I made my first translations forty-five years ago as a student in French and Spanish classes. Even then, before I had read a single theoretical word on the subject, my aim was to try to combine textual accuracy with poetic sympathy. The second of these, the desire to preserve the ardor of the original and to find in American English the formal ways of doing so, is more readily accomplished, or in any case attempted, with poems in one or another kind of free verse, and it was with such poems by Pedro Salinas and Pablo Neruda, poets of very different tonalities, that I began. I have taken the title of this book from the title of one of Salinas' poems, but the truth is that I don't feel much sympathy now for Salinas or Neruda and so have decided to include only two poems by Salinas and but one poem by Neruda of the many poems by both that I translated and published as a young man.

Translating poems in meter and rhyme is altogether something else. My first effort of this kind was Paul Valéry's "Les Pas," a poem I loved from the day I was asked to recite it in a fourth-year literature class. What I have learned over the years in translating metrical and rhymed poetry, that it requires not just skill and hard work but patience and even imperturbability, I got my first sense of in rendering Valéry's poem. By the time I had gone on to the trials of translating sonnets by Borges, Sor Juana Inés de la Cruz, and Salvador Díaz Mirón I'd read many essays on translation, including the one by Nabokov with the scarifying jingle, "Rhyme rhymes with crime." Against this stricture was Joseph Brodsky's joke, "international legislation should be introduced to prohibit the translation of classical verse into free verse."

I have always sided with Brodsky, if not the notion of international legislation, and have even given lectures endorsing his general position in the continuing and vexatious debate on how to translate "classical verse," for I am in total agreement with something he wrote in a different essay, "Verse meters in themselves are kinds of spiritual magnitudes for which nothing can be substituted." Still, for me translation has less to do with prose arguments than with poetic practice. If I can't stand with Nabokov, it's really because his translation of *Eugene Onegin* is unreadable. My touchstone for translation is Elizabeth Bishop's "Sonnet of Intimacy," her rendering of a poem by Vinicius de Moraes, which I first read in the early 1970s, a poem as witty and beautiful in English as, I am told by Brazilian friends, it is in de Moraes' Brazilian Portuguese. Almost as good as Bishop's translation are Pound's "Alba" (langue d'oc), Carolyn Kizer's "Tu Fu to Li Po" (Tu Fu), and Dom Moraes' "A Room by the Sea" (Yehuda Amichai). I have taken heart from these translations as testaments to the possibility of doing, and doing very well, what is often said to be impossible and so better off not tried.

Writers on translation routinely take up, as I have done just now, the matter of how, but what of why? Why did I translate the poems in this book? Money was a few times a reason, but a small one, for the money was small. Friendship was a keener reason. On several occasions I had the pleasure of sitting at tables with friends, colleagues, and one student who either knew a language I didn't know (Gu Zhen provided me with a trot of Li Bai's poem) or knew one much better than I did: Tatyana Amelina made paraphrases of seven early poems by Brodsky, four of which are here; Pascale Torracinta helped with the two Bonnefoy poems; and Marco Sonzogni and I worked by e-mail on Primo Levi, Marco in New Zealand, I in New England. A third motive was to bring over into English a kind of poem that English lacks; this was especially the case with Montale, Levi, and Brodsky. Fourth, several times I thought, immodestly, that I could do better than previous translators. A fifth motive was to say something about myself under the over of a translation, a device I discovered in Pound, as when in Canto I he writes of Elpenor, the youngest and least clever of Odysseus' crew, "A man of no fortune, and with a name to come," who is surely Pound himself. My two Poundian riffs are the versions of Catullus' Carmina 101 and the old English "Deor." The reader will see at once the use to which I put the first, but it needs to be said that I translated "Deor" after losing a job I was angry at losing. I felt it would be undignified to say that in a poem of my own, so I resorted, too obscurely I know, to an old poem both anonymous and, in its alliterative mode and historical references, remote.

Finally, first and last, I translated these poems because I liked them and wanted to convey that feeling and the emotions of the poems themselves in my language.

April 11, 2017

Elegy

Having driven two hundred miles through towns
of strangers, by cabins, trailers, Mormon outposts,
I have come, brother, to your mountain grave,
a month too late to do my part in the service,
and years too late to set things right between us.
What words are there after so long a silence—
the need to make a living took me from you,
and then the life you chose took you from me?
Let a few wildflowers and an old love be all,
brother, you have from me forever. Farewell.

Caius Valerius Catullus
Rome
84 B.C.–54 B.C.
(exact dates uncertain)

Seeing a Friend Off

Green hills head north from the city.
Clear water winds east from the wall.

Here, we say *so long!*—a single sail
setting out over two thousand miles.

A scudding cloud 's a traveler's mind,
the sun at evening a friend we've loved.

Your hand in the air, you turn to go.
Your horse's whinny goes on and on.

Li Bai
China
701–762

Deor

Wayland in Varmland
suffered adversities,
that strong-minded man
knew misery.
Bitter setbacks, pains
of winter cold, these
were his companions.
His truck was with trouble
after Nithhad had done
the violence to him—
hacking his hamstrings,
hobbling the better man.
    —That was endured;
    so may this be.

Beadohilde despaired
when her brothers were butchered,
but when she was sure
she carried a child—
that was what wrecked her.
She couldn't conceive
of a future.
    —That was endured;
    so may this be.

We've all of us heard
how the Geat loved Mathilde,
loved her without limit,
loved with such love
his sleep was shattered.
    —That was endured;
    so may this be.

Thirty years Theodric
ruled the Maeringa's town.
The facts are all known.
    —That was endured;
    so may this be.

We all know of Eormanric
and his wolflike ways—
subjugating subjects
the length of Gottland.
He was a cruel king!
Men sat unmoving,
shackled to sorrow,
thinking just one thing—
to cut the king down.
    —That was endured;
    so may this be.

Of myself I'll say this:
I was once the poet
of the Heodingas,
dear to my lord.
My name was Deor.
Winter to winter
I had a good holding,
a lavishing lord.
Now one Heorrenda,
a masterly man,
finds praise in the place
until lately my lord
gave to me.
    —That was endured;
    so may this be.

Anonymous
England
c. 850

To Hope

Green hypnotist of every human life,
Mad hope! The gilded frenzy every man
Is swept away by day by day, the strife
Of dreaming you'll win wealth because you can.

The world's soul; flourishing senility;
The happy remedy for age's sorrow;
The day the lucky know will be today,
And the unlucky think will be tomorrow.

Let those whose spectacles of green dye
The world so that it meets all their demands,
Invoke your name, who need your light so much;

But as for me, unsure of fortune, I
Will keep my eyes well shaded by my hands,
And see alone the things that I can touch.

Sor Juana Inés de la Cruz
New Spain
1651–1695

Saturday in the Village

As the sun sets
the girl comes home from the country,
carrying a bundle of grass
and a handful of roses and violets.
With these, the custom is, she gets
ready for tomorrow, the holiday,
adorning her breast and hair.
On the steps with her neighbors
the old woman sits spinning, her face
to the disappearing day,
and tells the story of her good time
when she'd adorn herself
and, still slender and full of grace,
dance the night away with those
who were her friends when she was lovely.
Now the air darkens,
the sky turns blue, and shadows fall
already from hills and roofs
in the whitening new moon.
Now the bell gives a sign
of the holiday to come:
and at that sound you would say
the heart is comforted.
The swarm of children
in the little square, shouting
and leaping here and there,
makes a happy noise.
And meanwhile the gardener goes,
whistling, to his meager meal,
thinking ahead to his day of rest.

Then, when every other light is spent,
and everything else is silent,
you hear the rapping hammer, the saw
of the carpenter, who stays up
in his closed shop in the lamplight
and hurries, pushing himself
to finish his work before dawn.

Of the seven days this day
is the day for thanksgiving.
Tomorrow the hours will bring
boredom and sadness,
and everyone will return
to the thoughts of the usual labor.

Playful boy,
this flowering time
is like a day of joy,
a cloudless day that heralds
the holiday of your life.
Be glad, my little boy.
It's a sweet state, a happy season.
I won't say more—only
this holiday that is about to come
let it not be heavy for you.

Giacomo Leopardi
Italy
1798–1837

The Infinite

I've always loved this hill off by itself
and this hedge screening off so much of all
there is out there to the horizon line.
But sitting here now, gazing out again,
I'm filled with a new sense of boundless space
and more-than-human silences and stillness,
and for a while my heart is not alarmed.
And my ear to the wind riffling the plants
I find myself comparing it with that
infinite silence, and I think again
of the eternal, of seasons past
and the too-present present and its sound.
So in this immensity I drown.
And going under 's easeful in this sea.

Giacomo Leopardi

To Himself

Now, worn-out heart,
you'll rest for good, the last deception dead
that I believed was deathless. Dead.
I'm sure
not just the hope, but the desire
for sweet illusions is all gone.
So rest for good.
You've had enough excitement. Nothing 's worth
all that you've suffered, nothing 's good enough
on the whole earth.
This life is bitter, tedious,
and never any better. The world 's shit.
So take your rest.
The one thing that's in store for us
is death. Show your contempt for it
and nature's brutal power that,
though hidden, governs everything—
the infinite vanity of everything.

Giacomo Leopardi

The Example

Exposed, the corpse was blackening like some
decaying fruit on the great roadside tree.
It hung as proof of an unjust decree,
and oscillated like a pendulum.

The tuft of hair on top, like a cock's comb,
indecent nakedness, and stuck-out tongue,
gave it a clownish look. I stood among
a gang of ragged kids who laughed at him.

And what was left on the green scaffold there—
the head bowed, mournful, scandalous, and shy—
discharged its stench into the swirling air,
a censer slowly swung above the road.

And the sun climbed up through a cloudless sky.
The fields were straight out of a Latin ode.

Salvador Díaz Mirón
Mexico
1853-1928

The Steps

Your steps, born of my silence,
Godly, familiar, slow,
Proceed, mute and cold,
To the bed of my vigilance.

Shadow and person, divine, complete,
They are so soft, your reticent steps!
God! All the gifts that I imagine
Come to me on those naked feet.

And if, with your ready lips,
You are preparing to appease
The life within my thoughts
With the sustenance of a kiss,

Do not hasten such tenderness,
Sweetness of being and not being:
I have lived for you by waiting,
And my heart was but your steps.

Paul Valéry
France
1871–1945

A Child's Dream

Bright night
of the fiesta and moon,
night of my dreams,
night of happiness!
(My soul is mist
that was light today,
and my hair
was not yet black.)
The youngest of the fairies
took me in his arms
to the fiesta of joy
that blazed in the streets.
There under the pulsing
of lamps and torches
love was uncoiling
his skein of dances,
and in that night
of the fiesta and moon,
night of my dreams,
night of happiness,
the youngest of the fairies
was kissing my forehead . . .
with his lovely hand
waving goodnight . . .
Every rosebush
was yielding its fragrance,
every lover
was unfolding to love.

Antonio Machado
Spain
1875–1939

Light of my soul, heavenly light,
lighthouse, torch, star, sun . . .
Every man goes groping in the dark,
and carries a lantern on his back.

Antonio Machado

The Goat

I've talked with a goat.
She was tethered
alone in a meadow.
Stuffed with grass, rain-
soaked, bleating.

That bleating on and on
was brother of my sorrow.
So I responded, first as a joke,
then because sorrow is eternal
and speaks in a voice that never varies.
I heard that voice
in the moaning of a solitary goat.

In a goat with a Semitic face
I heard a cry against every evil,
the crying of every life.

Umberto Saba
Italy
1883–1957

In Memory

Mohammed Sceab
was his name

Descended from a line
of nomadic emirs
a suicide
because
he had no country

He loved France
and changed his name

He was Marcel
but not French
though he no longer knew
how to live
in a tent of his own
listening to the melody
of the Koran
sipping coffee

And he didn't know
how to free
the song
of his abandonment

I accompanied him
with the woman who ran the hotel
where we lived
in Paris
at number 5 rue de Carmes
dull downhill alley

He lies
in the cemetery in Ivry
a suburb
that always looks
like the day
when a fair
is dismantled

And it's possible
only I
know that he lived

Giuseppe Ungaretti
Egypt, France, Italy
1888–1970

I Cannot Give You More

I cannot give you more.
I am not more than I am.

Oh, how I'd like to be
sand and sun in summer.
You'd stretched out like flame
there in your rest,
and when you left
you'd leave me with your body, an imprint
precious, flushed, unforgettable.
And with you you'd take
my slow kiss, a dark color
spreading over you
from head to foot,
a tan.

And oh, how I'd like to be
quilted silk, thin glass, or sandalwood
that keeps its fragrance
here, and its color,
though made a thousand miles away!
To be the stuff that pleases you,
that you touch every day,
and that you see without looking
around you—
necklace, flask, old silk—
the things that when they are missing
you ask, "Where can it be?"

And oh, how I'd like to be
a joy above all others,
the only joy, the one
in which you'd always rejoice!

A love, a single love:
the love with which you'd be in love!

But
I am not more than I am.

Pedro Salinas
Spain
1891–1951

The Truth of Two

As he lived by day, and only one day,
he could see nothing more than the light.
He imagined
that everything was light and sun and lasting
joy, that the birds
never stopped flying, and that the yeses
that the mouths said
gave way to no other side. The inexorable
decline of the sun towards its death,
the lengthening of the shadows,
seemed like innocent play to him,
never the presage, the slow triumph, of the dark.
And that space of being
measured from dawn to dusk
by the light,
he took for life.
His last smile showed the world
his faith that life was light,
day,
and clarity in which he existed.
He never saw the stars, ignorant
of those numberless hearts,
under the great blue sky that trembles with them.

She, yes.
She was born at the advent of night,
the daughter of the first shadow,
and in the night she lived.
She never suffered from colors
nor from the light's implacable cold.
Sheltered
in the vast, warm darkness,
her soul never knew
what the dark was, because she lived in it.
She died pure, unaware of exact
forms, distances, those inequalities
between straight lines and curves, blood and snow,
impossible, luckily,
in that absolute justice of the night.
And she saw the stars that he didn't see.

That's why
you and I, taking pity
on each one's solitary happiness,
have raised them up from their rest
and their living by halves.
And from now on they live in us, wounded, yes,
he by shadow and she by light;
and they know the blood and sorrows
that each day opens in the night and each dusk
in the breast of the day, and the sadness
of losing the light that doesn't stay,
and the joy of waiting for that which will come.

You, deceived
by clarity, and I by darkness,
so long as we walked alone,
have delivered ourselves, in exchanging
error for error, to the tragic truth
called the world, earth, love, destiny.
And the fatal face of it all we can see
in what I have given you and you given me.
At our love's birth there was born for each
the other's terrible, necessary side,
the light, the darkness.
The two of us go towards it. Never again alone.
The world, the truth of two, the fruit of two,
the paradisaic truth, the bitter apple,
attained only in the total tasting
when all innocence ends,
both of the day itself and the night by itself.
When cast on the sin
of living
in love with living, loving each other,
we must fight the fight that fulfills
those who have lost a bright paradise
or a paradise of darkness,
to discover another eden
where lights and shadows come, and where the mouth,
in encountering a kiss, encounters at last
the world's terrible roundness.

Pedro Salinas

To pass the noon, intent and pale,
beside a scorching orchard wall,
and hear in the dry thorny brake
clicking thrushes, a rustling snake.

On the cracked ground or in the vetch
to spy on the red ants in files
that now break up and now crisscross
the pinnacles of little piles.

To see through leaves the distantly
palpitating scaly sea
as all at once from the bald peaks
rise the cicadas' tremulous screaks.

And walking in the dazzling sun
to feel with sad amazement
how all we are and go through 's in
this following a wall up on

the top of which jagged bits of bottles run.

Eugenio Montale
Italy
1896–1981

The House of the Customs Men

You don't remember the house of the customs men
on the hillside above the cliff overhanging the reef.
Desolate, it has waited for you since the evening when
the swarm of your thoughts entered it
and paused, irresolute.

Southwest winds have lashed the old walls for years
and the sound of your laughter has lost its gaiety.
The compass for no reason at all goes crazy,
and the dice come up numbers no one guesses.
You don't remember; another time confuses
your memory; a thread is being lost.

I hold an end of it still; but the house
draws away and the smoke-blackened weathercock
on the rooftop whirls unpitying.
I'm holding an end; but you stay alone,
not breathing here in the dark.

Oh the fleeing horizon! where the light
of a tanker rarely flashes.
Is there a way through here? (The sea still crashes
against the crumbling cliff.)
You don't remember the house of this evening of mine.
And I don't know who goes and who remains.

Eugenio Montale

Xenia I

1

Dear little insect
whom we called Mosca—I don't know why—
this evening just before dark
as I was reading Deutero-Isaiah
you reappeared at my side,
but not having your glasses
you couldn't see me,
and without their glinting
I couldn't be sure
it was you in the dark.

2

Without your glasses or antennae,
a poor insect who had wings
only in imagination,
a Bible coming unbound
and largely unreliable,
the black of night, a lightning flash,
a thunderclap, and then
no storm. Can it be
you were gone so quickly
without saying a word?
But it's ridiculous to think
that you still had lips.

3

At the Saint James in Paris I'll have to ask
for a single room (they don't like
the odd guest). And also at your faux
Byzantium hotel in Venice;
and then immediately go down to find
the switchboard operators' cubbyhole—
those girls who were always your friends;
only to give up again—
the telephone connection lost—

the desire of having you back,
if only in one habit or gesture.

4

For the afterlife we had devised
a whistle, a sign of recognition.
I'm trying variations of it in the hope
we're all already dead without knowing it.

5

I've never understood
whether I was your dog,
faithful or sick with distemper,
or you were mine.
To others you were a myopic insect
at a loss in the blah blah
of high society. They were naïve,
those clever ones. They didn't know
they were your laughingstock,
that even in the dark you made them out,
unmasking them
with that infallible sense of yours,
your bat radar.

6

It never crossed your mind to write prose or verse
and so leave behind you traces of yourself.
That was your charm and then my self-disgust.
It was also my fear—
that you'd drive me back
into the croacking mire
of the neoteroi.

7

The self-pity, endless pain and anguish
of one who worships this world and hopes without hope
for another . . . (Who dares to speak of another world!).

"Strange piety . . . " (Azucena, Act II).

8

Your speech, so sparing and unguarded,
remains the one thing that satisfies me.
But the accent is different, the color changed.
I'll get accustomed to hearing you or deciphering you
in the ticking of the teletype,
in the shifting smoke from my Brissago cigars.

9

Listening was the only way you had of seeing.
Now the phone bill is down to next to nothing.

10

"Did she pray?" "Yes, she prayed to St Anthony
because he helps to find
lost umbrellas and other things
from St Hermes' closet."
"Only for that?" "Also for her dead
and for me."
"That's enough," said the priest.

11

To remember your tears (mine numbered twice as many)
isn't to blot out your burst of laughter.
They were like a deposit on your private
Last Judgment, which unfortunately never came to pass.

12

Spring comes along at a mole's pace.
I won't hear you any more talking of poisonous
antibiotics, the spike in your femur,
the patrimony you were fleeced of
by a predatory nonentity.

Spring approaches with its thick fogs,
longer days, and unbearable hours.
I won't hear you any more struggling
with time, ghosts, or the logistical
problems of summer.

13

Your brother died young; you were
the disheveled girl who looks out at me
"posed" in an oval portrait.
He wrote music, unpublished, unheard,
now buried in a trunk or rotted away.
Perhaps someone is reinventing it
unwittingly, if what 's written is written.
I loved him without having known him.
Except for you, no one remembered him.
I made no inquiries; now there's no point.
After you I'm the only one left
for whom he existed. But it's possible,
you know, to love a shade,
being shades ourselves.

14

They say that mine
is a poetry of not belonging.
But if it was yours it was someone's—
you who are no longer form but essence.
They say that the highest poetry
praises the Oneness of life as it flees,
denying that the tortoise
is quicker than lightning.
Only you knew that motion
is not different from stasis,
the void is fullness and a clear sky
the most diffuse of clouds.
So I understand better your long journey
imprisoned in bandages and plasters.
And yet it doesn't comfort me
to know that as one or as two
we are a single thing.

Xenia II

1

Death didn't concern you.
Though among the dead were your two dogs
and the asylum doctor known as the Demented Uncle,
as well as your mother with her "specialty"
of rice and frogs—a Milanese triumph—
and even your father, who evening and morning
watches me from a miniature
portrait on the wall.
Despite all this, death didn't concern you.

It was I who attended the funerals,
unseen in a taxi standing a ways off
to avoid tears and irritations. Not even
life and its exhibitions of vanity and greed
mattered to you, and so
so much less the universal gangrenes
that transform men into wolves.

A tabula rasa; except
that there came a point, incomprehensible to me,
and this point *concerned you*.

2

You were too often reminded (I seldom was) of Herr Cap.
"I saw him on Ischia, on the bus, maybe twice.
He's a lawyer in Klagenfurt, the one who sends his best wishes.
He's supposed to come for a visit."

And finally he comes. I tell him everything: he's dumbfounded.
It seems it's a catastrophe for him as well. For a while he says nothing.
Then he stands up, mumbling and stiff, and assures me
he'll send his best wishes.
It's strange
how the most unlikely people turned out to understand you.
Counselor Cap. What a name! And Celia. What became of her?

3

For a long time the shoehorn was missing,
that rusted tin horn we took with us everywhere,
though to carry so indecorous a thing
among the tombac and stucco seemed indecent.
It must have been at the Danieli that I forgot
to put it back into the suitcase or small bag.
I'm sure that Hedia the chambermaid threw it
into the Grand Canal. And how could I have written
that I was searching for three inches of tin?
Prestige (*ours*) had to be saved
and Hedia, the faithful, had saved it.

4

Uncannily
escaping from the jaws of Etna
or the teeth of ice,
you came out
with incredible revelations.

Mangano, the good surgeon, witnessed one:
you exposed him as the Black Shirts' cudgel,
and he smiled.

That was you: even on the edge of the abyss
sweetness and terror in a single note.

5

I've descended, your arm in mine, almost a million stairs
and now that you're not here a void opens at every step.
Even so, our long journey was brief.
Mine still goes on, though I no longer feel the need
for connections, reservations,
mix-ups, the scorn of those who believe
that reality is what one sees.

I've descended millions of stairs, your arm in mine,
not, of course, because four eyes see better than two.
I descended them with you because I knew

that between us the only true pupils,
however clouded over, were yours.

6

The wine steward poured you a little
Inferno. And you, frightened: "Must I drink it?
Isn't it enough to be there slowly burning?"

7

"I've never been sure of being in the world."
"How clever," you responded. "And me?"
"Oh, you've nibbled at the world's edges,
if only in homeopathic doses. But I . . . "

8

"And Paradise? Does paradise exist?"
"I believe so, Signora,
But no one drinks sweet wines any more."

9

Nuns and widows, those deadly,
malodorous, professional mourners,
you wouldn't let yourself look at them.
You were sure that even he
who has a thousand eyes
turns away from them.
The all-seeing, him . . . judicious,
you didn't call him god,
not even with a small g.

10

I'd been looking a long time
when finally I found you in a bar
on the Avenida de Liberdada. You didn't know
a single world of Portuguese—or rather,
knew a single word: Madeira. And a small glass came
along with a plate of shrimp.

That evening they likened me to illustrious
Lusitanians with unpronounceable names
and, to top it off, to Carducci.
I saw you, unimpressed, hidden in a crowd,
laughing so hard you were crying;
bored, perhaps, but with compunction.

11

Resurfacing out of an infinity of time,
Celia the Philippine called
just to see how you were doing.
"I believe she's well," I said,
"maybe better than before." "What? You believe?
Isn't she there?" "Maybe more than before, but . . .
Celia, try to understand . . ."
    On the other end of the line,
in Manila or some other
name on the map, stammering
stymied even her. And she slammed down the phone.

12

The hawks
always too far away for you,
you seldom saw them really well.
The one at Etretat that watched
the clumsy flights of its young.
Two others in Greece, on the road to Delphi,
a scuffle of soft feathers, two beaks,
young, ardent and harmless.

You liked life ripped to shreds,
whatever broke free of its unbearable
form.

13

I have hung up in my room the daguerreotype
of your father as a child: it's more than a century old.
In the absence of my own (a confused thing),
I try to reconstruct, unsuccessfully, your pedigree.

We aren't horses, our ancestors' lines
aren't in the books. Those who presumed
to know such things did not themselves exist,
nor did we for them. And so? It's still the case
that something happened, perhaps a nothing
that is everything.

14

The flood has covered the clutter of furniture,
papers, and paintings that filled
a basement locked with a double lock.
Perhaps the red moroccos fought blindly,—
and so too the endless dedications of Du Bos,
the wax seal with Ezra's beard,
Alain's Valéry, the first edition
of Canti Orifice—not to mention some shaving
brushes, a thousand trifles, and all
your brother Silvio's music.
Ten, twelve days in the atrocious hold
of naphtha and dung. Surely they suffered
a lot before losing their identity.
I too am encrusted up to the neck,
but my civil status was dubious from the start.
It's not the muck that besieges me, but the events
of a reality that's unbelievable
and never believed in.
In the face of it all, courage
was the first gift you gave me,
and perhaps you didn't know it.

Eugenio Montale

In the Smoke

How many times I waited for you at the station
in the cold, the fog. I'd stroll up and down
coughing, buying unspeakable newspapers,
smoking the Giubas later banned by that fool
the Minister of Tobacco.
Sometimes the wrong train, or one added late
or out of service. I'd inspect
the baggage cars, certain that I'd see
your bags and, behind them, you.
Then finally you appeared. It's a memory
among so many others, and it haunts my dreams.

Eugenio Montale

Late at Night

A colloquy with the shades
isn't something for the telephone.
Our mute conversations are carried on
without a portable or loudspeaker.
And yet we attend to words
even when they don't concern us—
picked up by mistake by an operator
and connected to someone
who isn't there,
who doesn't hear.
One time they came from Vancouver
late at night
while I was holding for Milan. I was surprised
at first, then hoped the strange mistake
would go on. One voice from the Pacific,
the other from the lagoon. And that time
the two voices spoke freely as never before.
For a while nothing happened.
We assured the operator that everything
was all right, perfect, and could—
in fact, must—continue. We never knew
who paid the bill for that miracle.
And I don't recall a word of it.
The time zone was different, the other
voice wasn't here, I wasn't there for her,
even the languages were jumbled, a pot-
pourri of jargon, swearing, and laughter.
Now after so many years the other voice
doesn't remember it and maybe believes I'm dead.
I believe she is the dead one.
For a time anyway she was alive
and was never aware of it.

Eugenio Montale

Venetian Prose

Farfarella, the garrulous porter,
only following orders,
said he was forbidden to disturb
the man of bullfights and safaris.
I plead with him: I'm a friend of Pound
(I exaggerate a little) and deserve
special treatment. If he would only . . .
He lifts the phone,
speaks, listens, speaks again, and then
Hemingway the bear steps into the trap.
He's still in bed. In his hairy head
the eyes and eczema are glistening holes.
Two or three empty bottles of Merlot,
the *avant-garde* of a lot to come.
Down in the restaurant everyone 's at dinner.
We speak not of him but of our dear friend
Adrienne Monnier, rue de l'Odeon,
Sylvia Beach, Larbaud, the roaring thirties
and the braying fifties. Paris. London, a pigsty.
New York, *stinking*, pestilent. He says
nothing of shooting in marshes, wild ducks, or girls,
nothing even of the idea of a book about such things.
We make a list of friends we have in common,
some names I don't know. Everything 's rotten, corrupt.
Almost in tears, he asks me not to send him
others of my kind, especially intelligent ones.
Then he gets up, wraps himself in a robe,
and, embracing me, shows me to the door.
He lived for a few more years and dying twice
had a chance to read his obituaries.

Eugenio Montale

Sorapis, 40 Years Later

I've never liked the mountains much,
and I detest the Alps. I've never seen
the Andes or Cordilleras.
Only the Sierra de Guadarrama enraptured me,
gentle in its ascent and with fallow deer
on the peaks—stags,
according to the tourist brochure.
Only the electric air of the Engadine
took our breath away, my little insect,
but it wasn't so rich that it made us say
hic manebimus.
Among the lakes only that of Sorapis
was a great discovery. It had the solitude
of marmots more heard of than glimpsed
and the air of Celestials. But what a road
for getting there! The first time
I took it alone in order to see
if your eyes could penetrate the clouds
zigzagging among the high slaps of ice.
And how long it was! and made easy only
in the first stretch, a dark stand of conifers,
by the ringing alarm of jays.
Then holding you by the hand, I guided you
up to the top, an empty hut.
That was our lake: a few spans of water,
two lives much too young to be old
and much too old to feel we were young.
We discovered then what age is.
It has nothing to do with time,
but is something that says, that makes us say,
we are here, a miracle
that cannot repeat itself. By comparison,
youth is the vilest of deceptions.

Eugenio Montale

Heroism

Clizia used to suggest that I join
the partisans in Spain, and more than once I saw myself
dead in Guadalajara or an illustrious survivor
barely able to stand after years in the galleys.
But nothing like that ever occurred: fate denied me
even the rally where my torrents of words
were rewarded with fame and future assignments.
But where have I seen action, I, who do not love
the flocking of the inane and refugees?
I remember one thing: a prisoner of mine
who had a Rilke in his pocket and we were friends
for a few moments; and of no moment then
were the labors, thudding shells, and annoying
ticking of snipers.
Or so it seemed—though not to her
who didn't love homelands and had one only by chance.

Eugenio Montale

The End of '68

I've contemplated from the moon (or almost)
this modest planet that holds
philosophy, theology, politics,
pornography, literature, and sciences
self-evident and arcane. Inside it all there's man,
and I am one of them. And it's all very strange.

In a few hours it will be night and the year
will end with explosions of spumanti
and fireworks. Perhaps with bombs or worse,
but not where I am. If somebody dies
it's of no consequence to anyone so long as it's
a stranger and far away.

Eugenio Montale

The Enigmas

I who am he who now is singing will
Tomorrow be a mystery, the dead,
Lodged in a magical orb life has fled,
Without before or after, timeless, still.
So says the mystic. I believe that I'm
Unworthy of hell's fires or God's glory,
But I make no prediction. A man's story,
Like Proteus's shape, changes all the time.
What winding labyrinth, what whiteness blind
With light, will be my fate when the last breath
Of this adventure failing me I find
The curious experience of death?
I want to drink its pure oblivion—
To be forever, never to have been.

Jorge Luis Borges
Argentina
1899–1986

Spinoza

The Jew's translucent hands in the earth's shade
Polish the lenses, and the afternoon
That's dying out is cold, and men afraid.
(This being just like any afternoon.)
The hands, the sky the color of hyacinth
Until it whitens at the ghetto's wrist,
For this calm soul almost do not exist
As he imagines one clear labyrinth.
Fame does not trouble him, but only seems
A dream reflected in another's dreams.
A man the love of maidens never jars,
He's free of metaphor and myth to sit
Grinding a stubborn lens: the infinite
Map of the One whose being is His stars.

Jorge Luis Borges

To Silvestre Revueltas of Mexico, In His Death

When a man like Silvestre Revueltas
goes back into the ground at last,
there is a rumor, a wave's
voice that makes known his departure.
The tiny roots tell the grain, "Silvestre has died,"
and the wheat carries his name to the slopes
and then the bread knows it.
Soon every tree in America knows it,
and the frozen flowers of our arctic region.

Drops of water transmit it,
and the indomitable rivers of Araucania
take notice of it.
From glacier to lake, from lake to plant,
from plant to fire, and fire to smoke,
everything that burns, sings, blooms, dances, and lives again,
everything that lasts, high and deep in our America,
welcomes it:
pianos and birds, dreams and disturbances, the quivering net
that unites in air all our weathers,
tremble and translate the funeral chorus:
Silvestre has died, Silvestre has entered his fullest music
in his sonorous silence.

Brother of the earth, son of the earth, from here you pass into Time.
From now on your name full of music will fly up as though from a field
whenever it touches your country,
with a sound never heard, with the sound, brother, of you.

Your heart like a cathedral covers us in this instant, like the sky,
and your song, loud and magnificent, your volcanic tenderness,
fills to the roof like a burning statue.
Why has your life run out? Why
has it spilled
like blood into this cup? Why
have you searched
like a blind angel, groping against dark doors?

Oh, but out of your name there comes music,
and out of your music, as though out of a market,
there come wreaths of fragrant laurel,
and apples of perfume and symmetry.

On this solemn day of departure you are the departed,
but you no longer hear.
Your noble face is missing as if a man were missing
a great tree in the middle of his house.

Yet the light that we see from now on is another light,
the street that doubles back is a new street,
the hand that we touch from now on has your force,
everything takes its strength in your rest,
and your purity will climb out of the stones
to show us the clarity of your hope.

Lie still, brother, your day has ended.
With your sweet and powerful soul you filled it
with a light more luminous than the day's light,
and with a sound blue like the voice of heaven.
Your brothers and friends have asked me
to say your name again in the air of America
so that the bull of the pampa will know it, and the snow,
so that the sea will take it under, and the wind discuss it.
Now the stars of America are your country,
and from now on the Earth without doors is your home.

Pablo Neruda
Chile
1904–1973

Crescenzago

The sun comes up even in Crescenzago,
though perhaps you thought that impossible—
comes up and looks around for a meadow
or a forest or a lake or a hill,
and not finding one, with a scowl
sucks the mist out of the Naviglio canal.

The wind whirls down off the mountain peaks,
runs free across the endless plateau.
But when it catches sight of these smokestacks,
it turns and flees as far as it can go,
because the smoke is so black and toxic
the wind is afraid that it will choke.

The old women sit wasting hour after hour,
and count the raindrops as they fall.
The faces of the children have the color
of the streets covered with dust particles,
and the women never sing here,
but the trams hiss, hoarse and regular.

At Crescenzago there's a window
and behind it a girl growing pale.
With a needle and thread in her right hand,
she sews and rechecks the clock on the wall,
and at the whistle blaring she is off,
she sighs and weeps, and this is her life.

When the siren wails just after dawn
they scramble out of their tousled beds,
and with eyes dark-ringed and ears stunned
go down to the streets still chewing food.
They pump up the tires on their bikes
and light their cigarette butts.

From morning till night they make sure
the panting black stonecrusher 's never still,
or all day long they monitor
the twitching hands on a dial.
On Saturday nights they make love
in the ditch the inspector lives above.

Primo Levi
February 1943
Italy
1919–1987

Singing

. . . But when we began to sing
Our songs, senseless and good,
It seemed that everything
Stood as it once had stood.

The days were merely days,
And seven made a week.
Killing we thought was wicked.
Of dying we didn't think.

The months sped by so fast,
With too many to come for complaints!
Again we were only young,
Not martyrs, the shamed, or saints.

We had these thoughts and others
For as long as we could sing.
But it's all hard to explain,
Being a cloudlike thing.

Primo Levi
January 3, 1946

Sunset at Fossoli

I know what it means not to return.
Through barbed wire I have seen
The sun go down and die,
And have felt my flesh torn
By an old poet's words:
"The sun may set and rise,
But we, contrariwise,
Sleep after our short light
One everlasting night."

Primo Levi
February 7, 1946

The Little Girl of Pompeii

Because everyone's anguish is our anguish, we
Go on reliving yours, thin little girl

Who held yourself convulsively to your mother
As though you wanted to be inside her again

When in the afternoon the sky turned black.
No use. Because the air becoming poison

Filtered to find you through the closed window
Of your peaceful, solidly built house, already

Made happy by your singing and shy smile.
Centuries have passed, the ash has petrified,

Imprisoning forever your soft limbs.
So you will remain among us, contorted chalk,

Endless agony, terrible testimony
To how little the gods care for our poor seed.

But nothing remains of your faraway sister,
The young Dutch girl walled up within four walls,

Who nevertheless wrote of her futureless youth.
Her mute dust has been scattered by the wind,

Her brief life locked inside a worn-out notebook.
Nothing remains of the Hiroshima schoolgirl,

A wall shadow cast by the light of a thousand suns,
A victim sacrificed on the altar of fear.

You, powerful ones, owners of new poison,
Sad secret keepers of the definitive thunder,

The sky's afflictions are more than enough for us.
Before you push the button, stop and consider.

Primo Levi
November 20, 1978

Pliny

Don't hold me back, my friends, but let me sail.
I won't go far—only as far as the other shore.
I want to see up close that mottled cloud
Rising above Vesuvius, and discover
Where it is this strange light 's coming from.

Won't you go with me, nephew? Well, stay and study.
Transcribe those notes I left you yesterday.
Don't be afraid of the ash: ash from ashes,
We ourselves are ash: you remember Epicurus?
Quick, prepare the ship. Already night is falling.

Night at midday: a wonder never seen before.
Don't be afraid, sister. I am careful and competent.
The years that have stooped me haven't idly passed.
I'll soon be back. Just give me time enough
To row across, observe these things, and return.

That way I'll have a new chapter tomorrow
For my books, which I hope will live on
When for centuries the atoms of this old body
Have whirled loose in the vortices of the universe,
Or returned as an eagle, a young girl, or a flower.

Sailors, obey me: shove the ship out to sea.

Primo Levi
May 23, 1978

Brown Battalion

Is it possible to adopt a more absurd route?
In San Martino Street there is an anthill

Half a meter from the streetcar line,
And right there at the base of one of the rails

A long brown battalion of ants is unwinding.
Muzzle to muzzle one ant meets another,

Perhaps to learn news of their journeys or fortune.
In short, these stupid sisters

Nervous obstinate industrious
Have excavated their city inside our city,

Mapped out their line of tracks beside our tracks.
And they run over ours without suspecting,

Indefatigable in their precarious business,
Taking no notice . . .
                                        I don't want to write about it,

I don't want to write about this brown battalion.
I don't want to write about any brown battalion.

Primo Levi
August 13, 1980

Passover

Tell me: how does this night
Differ from all other nights?
How does this Passover
Differ from all other Passovers?
Light the candles, open the door
That the sojourner may come in,
Gentile or Jew.
The prophet might be wearing rags.
May he come in and sit down with us,
Listen, drink, sing, and rejoice in Passover.
May he eat the bread of affliction,
Lamb, sweet mortar paste, and bitter herbs.
This is the night of differences,
When we put our elbows on the table,
Because what's forbidden becomes permitted
So that evil may be translated into good.
We will spend the night telling stories
Of ancient events full of wonder,
And by drinking glasses of wine
We'll see the mountains come down like birds.
This night the wise, the wicked,
The naïve and the newborn
Ask the same questions,
And time turns round and runs backward,
Today refluxes yesterday,
Like a river flooding up from its delta.
Each of us has been in Egypt,
Has soaked straw and clay with our sweat,
And has crossed the sea on dry feet.
You, too, stranger.
This year in fear and shame,
Next year in virtue and justice.

Primo Levi
April 9, 1982

Wooden Heart

My next-door neighbor is robust: a horse
Chestnut tree in Re Umberto Street.

It's as old as I am, but doesn't show it.
It takes in sparrows and blackbirds and isn't ashamed.

In April it presses out buds and leaves,
Fragile flowers in May,

And in September husks with harmless thorns
And shiny tannic chestnuts inside the husks.

It's an impostor, but innocent, pretending
To be emulating its good mountain brother,

Lord of sweet fruits and precious mushrooms.
But its life is hard. Every five minutes

Trams No. 18 and 19 trample its roots.
Stunned by that, it grows bent to one side

As though it wanted to get out of here.
Year after year, it sucks in slow poisons

From the subsoil saturated with methane.
It gets its water from urinating dogs.

The wrinkles in its cork skin are chock-full
Of the septic dust swirling in the streets.

Beneath its bark, dead chrysalises hang,
Which never will change into butterflies.

Yet even so, in its tired wooden heart,
It feels and takes joy in the turning seasons.

Primo Levi
May 10, 1980

The Thaw

When the snow has melted entirely,
We will go looking for the old footpath
Now covered by the blackberry bushes
Behind the wall of the monastery.
Then all will be as it was formerly.

On either side, in the thick shrubbery,
We will find again a certain herb
Whose name I could never tell you.
I change it every Friday,
But forget it every Saturday.
I was told it is rare
And good for melancholy.

The ferns along the path's borders
Are as tender as small creatures:
They barely surface from the ground,
Curled in spirals, and yet
They are ready by now for their loves,
Alternate, green, and more intricate than ours.

Their germs are gnawing at what 's holding back
The males and females
In the rusty spore-sac.
They will burst out in the first downpour,
Aswim at the first drop,
Yearning and agile. Long live the married pairs!

We're tired of winter now.
Frost has done all that it could
To flesh, mind, mud, and wood.
May the thaw come and melt the memory
Of last year's snow.

Primo Levi
February 2, 1985

The Snail

Why hurry at all when you're so well protected?
Why should one place be better than another
As long as you're not without dampness and grass?
Why run, and run the risk of an accident,
When by retreating into yourself you're at peace?
And even if the world proves hostile then,
You seal yourself off from it silently
Behind your veil of clear innocuous chalk,
Denying the world, and denying yourself to it.
But when the meadow is watery with dew
Or rain has rendered the earth mild again,
Every route becomes your thoroughfare,
The paving beautiful shining slimy liquid,
Bridging leaf to leaf and stone to stone.
You navigate with care, secretly, safely,
Testing the way with telescopic eyes,
Graceful, filthy, logarithmic,
Until you find the other female/male,
And anxious, tensed, and pulsing from your shell,
You know the shy charms of ambiguous love.

Primo Levi
December 7, 1983

The Mouse

A mouse has got in, by who knows what hole,
Not silent, as they usually are,
But presumptuous, arrogant, and out to impress.
It was loquacious, flowery, cavalier:
It climbed on top of my bookshelf
And delivered a lecture to me,
Citing Plutarch, Nietzsche, and Dante:
That I shouldn't waste time,
Blah blah, that time flies,
And that time lost is lost for good,
And that time is money,
And that time waits for no man
Because life is short and art is long,
And at my back I always hear
Time's winged chariot hurrying near.
What nerve! What conceit!
He was boring me to tears.
What would a mouse know about time?
And a mouse that was wasting my time
With its barefaced rant.
If it's a mouse, let it lecture mice.
I told it to get lost.
I know very well what time is.
It comes up in lots of physic equations,
In some cases even squared
Or with a negative exponent.
I can look after my own problems.
I don't need anybody else's interference.
Charity begins at home.

Primo Levi
January 15, 1983

At Galvani's

My boss has a thing for frogs.
Every night he sends me down to the bank of the Rhone,
But he doesn't hand them over to Gegia for frying.
Instead of looking after his patients,
He hangs frogs from the balcony's iron railing,
Skins them, tortures them with a nail,
And spends his day watching them dance
While he composes letters in Latin.
Who knows what he hopes to get out of them!
Still, every night I have to go around
With a lantern, net, and basket.
I have to say, though, it isn't a new job.
Even the other one, the one from Scandiano,
Yes, him, the Abbot Spallanzani:
He, too, sent me for frogs.
But rather than hang them on a railing,
He'd mix the males and females together
And put tiny pantaloons on the males
So they could no longer fuck.
And then he claims to be a Christian!
Bosses are almost all insane.

Primo Levi
May 3, 1984

August

Who remains in the city in August?
Only the poor and the insane,
Old ladies left behind,
Pensioners with Pomeranians,
Thieves, here and there an aristocrat, and cats.
Along the deserted streets
You hear a percussive beat of heels
And you see women with plastic bags
Standing in the line of shade along the walls.
Under the fountain with the turret
In the green algaed pool
There's a middle-aged naiad
Ten and a half centimeters tall
With nothing on but a bra.
A few meters away,
Despite the well known prohibition,
Panhandling pigeons
Set upon you
And steal the bread out of your hand.
You hear in the sky the whoosh,
In exhausted flight, of the noonday demon.

Primo Levi
July 22, 1986

The Elephant

Dig and you'll find my absurd bones
In this spot down in the deep snow.
I was fed up with the load and the marching
And having to go without warmth and grass.
You'll find coins and Punic weapons
Under the avalanches: absurd, absurd!
That's what my story and History are: absurd.
What did Carthage and Rome matter to me?
Now my beautiful ivory, our pride,
Noble, sickle-shaped like the moon,
Lies splintered among the torrent's stones.
It wasn't meant to pierce breastplates
But to dig up roots and please our females.
We only fight for females,
And sensibly, without shedding blood.
Would you like to hear my story? It's brief.
The clever Indian lured and tamed me,
The Egyptian shackled and sold me,
The Phoenician covered me with weapons
And built a tower on my back.
It was absurd that I, a tower of flesh,
Invulnerable, mild, and intimidating,
Confined in these hostile mountains,
Slipped on your ice that I'd never seen before.
For us, when we fall, there is no salvation.
Some blind hero kept on trying to find
My heart with the point of his lance.
To these mountaintops, lurid in the sunset,
I trumpeted my useless
Dying bellow: absurd, absurd!

Primo Levi
March 23, 1984

Old Mole

What's so strange? I didn't like the sky.
So I chose to live alone and in the dark.
I developed good hands for digging,
Scooped, hooked, but sensitive and strong.
Now I travel sleeplessly,
Undetected under the fields
Where I feel neither heat nor cold
Nor wind rain day night snow
And where I do without my eyes.
I dig and discover succulent roots,
Tubers, rotting wood, stringy fungi,
And if a boulder blocks my way
I go around it, with some effort but unhurried
Because I always know where I want to go.
I find earthworms, larvae, and salamanders,
One time I came on a truffle,
Another time a snake, a good dinner,
And treasures buried by who knows whom.
I used to pursue females.
When I heard one scratching
I'd dig my way toward her.
Not now. If I hear something, I go the other way.
Though in the new moon I get excited
And then sometimes I like to
Pop up suddenly to scare the dogs.

Primo Levi
September 22, 1982

The Dromedary

So many disputes, lawsuits, and wars—what for?
You should try to imitate me.
No water? I do without it,
Careful only not to waste my breath.
No food? I dip into my hump.
When the time is propitious
Grow one yourselves.
And if the hump is flabby
All I need are weeds and straw.
Green grass is lechery and vanity.
Is my voice ugly? Usually I'm silent,
And if I bellow, nobody hears me.
Am I ugly? I'm pleasing to my female,
Who has an eye for quality
And gives the best milk ever.
Why not ask yours to do the same?
I am a servant, yes, but the desert is mine:
There is no servant without his own kingdom.
My kingdom is desolation.
It has no borders.

Primo Levi
November 24, 1986

Avigliana

A curse on those the full moon is lost on,
That comes only once a month.
A curse on this country,
On this dumb moon
That serene and brilliant shines
As if you were with me.

And there is even a nightingale
As in the books of a century ago;
But I made him fly off,
Far away, to the other side of the stream:
He is singing and I am alone,
And that isn't getting anywhere.

Lightning bugs, I let them stay
(There were a lot along the path):
Not that their name is nearly yours,
But they are such mild and dear creatures
That they make every worry disappear.
And if one day we should want to part,
And if one day we should care to marry,
I hope that day will be in June,
And there will be lightning bugs everywhere,
Like tonight, when you're not here.

Primo Levi
June 28, 1946

The Black Stars

No one should sing any more of love or war.

The order the cosmos was named for is gone.
The celestial legions are a monstrous blur.
The universe besieges us, blind and violent.
The serene sky is interspersed with dead suns,
Dense deposits of annihilated atoms.
Only desperate weight emanates from them—
Not energy, messages, particles, or light.
Light itself collapses from its own heaviness.
And all our human seed live and die for nothing.
And the skies spin round perpetually to no purpose.

Primo Levi
November 30, 1974

Samson

Son of a sterile mother,
I also was announced

By a messenger, a man
Of terrible countenance.

I was a child of the Sun,
And was myself the Sun.

I had the Sun's force focused
In my bull loins. Sun, beast,

I slew enemies by the thousands,
Battered down doors and broke chains,

Forced women, set fire to harvests,
Until Philistine Delilah

Sheared off my hair and strength,
And extinguished the light in my eyes.

Against darkness there is no fighting.
My hair has grown again,

And so has my animal force,
But not my joy in living.

Delilah

Samson of Timnah, rebel
Big talking earthshaking Judean,

Was in my delicate hands
As workable as clay.

It was easy to get out of him
The secret of his vain strength.

I flattered and cajoled him,
I had him sleep on my lap,

Still full of his foreign semen.
I blinded him, then sheared him,

Knocking out his kidneys.
My anger and my lust

Have never known such peace
As when I beheld him chained.

Not when I felt him inside me.
Let him go to his fate. I'm done.

Primo Levi
April 5, 1985

Hopkins Forest

I'd gone out
to get water from the well near the trees,
and was in the presence of another sky.
Gone were the constellations
of a moment before.
Three fourths of the firmament was empty,
the intensest black shone there alone,
though to the left, above the horizon,
in among the tops of the oaks,
was a mass of reddening stars
like firecoals, from which smoke even rose.

I went back inside
and re-opened the book on the table.
Page after page
there were only indecipherable signs,
clusters of forms without any sense,
although vaguely recurring,
and beneath them an abyssal white
as if what we call the spirit
were falling there, soundlessly,
like snow.
Still, I went on turning the pages.

Many years earlier,
in a train at the moment when the day rises,
between Princeton Junction and Newark,
—that is to say, two chance places for me,
two arrows fallen out of nowhere—
the passengers were reading, silent
in the snow that was sweeping the gray windows,
and suddenly,
in a newspaper open next to me—
a big photograph of Baudelaire,
a whole page,
as if the sky were emptying at the world's end
in recognition of the chaos of words.

I put together this dream and this memory
when I walked, all of one fall,

in woods where snow would soon triumph,
among the many signs we receive,
contradictorily,
from the world devastated by language.
The conflict between two principles,
it seemed to me, was nearing an end,
two lights were becoming one,
the lips of a wound closing.
The white mass of the cold was falling in gusts
on color, but a roof in the distance, a painted
board, standing against a gate,
was color still, and mysterious,
like someone coming out of a tomb, laughing,
and telling the world, "No, don't touch me."

Truly I owe a lot to Hopkins Forest.
I keep it on my horizon, in that place
where the visible gives way to the invisible
in the trembling of the blue in the distance.
I listen to it, amid other sounds,
and at times even, in summer,
kicking the dead leaves of other years
lying as if lit in the shade of oaks
grown densely among stones,
I stop: I believe that the ground is opening
to the infinite, that the leaves are falling into it
without hurry, or coming up again,
above and below no longer existing,
or sound, only the light
whispering of snowflakes that soon
multiply, draw closer, bind together—
and then I see again the whole other sky,
I enter for a moment the great snow.

Yves Bonnefoy
France
1923–2016

Lightning

It rained during the night.
The road has the smell of wet grass,
Then, again, the hand of the heat 's
On our shoulder, as if
To say time will take nothing from us.

But there
Where the field comes up against the almond tree,
See, a fallow dear has leaped
From yesterday to today through the leaves.

And we stop, it isn't of this world.

And I come close to you,
I finish breaking you off from the blackened trunk,
Branch, summer-lightning struck,
From which yesterday's sap, heavenly still, runs.

Yves Bonnefoy

The wind abandoned the woods
and rushed off to the sky.
It pushed aside the clouds
and then the white up high.

Now the woods stand alone,
cold, as in lasting dark,
with no desire for wind
and no distinguishing mark.

Joseph Brodsky
Soviet Union, United States
1940–1996

For Schoolchildren

You know, I try, when darkness falls,
to estimate to some degree—
by marking off the grief in miles—
the distance now from you to me.

And all the figures change to words:
confusion, which begins at A,
and hope, which starts at B, move towards
a terminus (you) far away.

Two travelers, each one with a light,
move in the darkness, silent, dumb.
The distance multiplies all night.
They count on meeting in the sum.

Joseph Brodsky

I held those shoulders in my arms, and glanced
behind her back to see what was revealed,
and saw a pulled-out chair just as it chanced
to merge with the illuminated wall.
The single high-watt light bulb that was on
made the worn furniture look touch-and-go.
The leather sofa in the corner shone;
its nut-brown cast an almost yellow glow.
The tabletop was bare; the parquet gleamed;
the stove loomed darkly; on the dusty wall
a landscape froze. Right then the sideboard seemed
the only thing with any life at all.
But a moth started circling the room,
freeing my gaze from immobility.
And if a ghost once made this place his home
he disappeared—abandoned it to me.

Joseph Brodsky

Odysseus to Telemachus

My Telemachus,
                                        The Trojan war
is done. Who won . . . is anybody's guess.
Presumably the Greeks: who else but Greeks
could hurl so many corpses out of houses?
But either way, the homeward-heading road 's
turned out to be too long, as though Poseidon,
while we were wasting time, extended space.
I don't know where I am or what's ahead—
some filthy island, bushes, buildings, stones,
great grunting pigs, a garden gone to weeds,
some sort of queen, and grass . . . Telemachus,
all islands look alike to one who's traveled
so long; and the brain trips up counting waves;
the eyes, polluted with horizon, blear;
and liquefying flesh clogs up the ears.
I don't remember how the war turned out . . .
I don't remember now how old you are.

Grow, Telemachus, my son, grow big.
The gods alone know if we'll meet again.
It's years already since you were that infant
I reined the oxen in to save. If not
for Palamedes, we'd have lived together.
But maybe he was right: apart from me,
you will be saved from Oedipal desires,
and, my Telemachus, have sinless dreams.

Joseph Brodsky
1972

What do the bushes say to the wind,
their leaves are poor?
Their speeches are probably simple,
but seem obscure.
Outvoicing the clanging bucket,
the creaking chair—
"Today you're stronger. Yesterday
you blew more fair."
The wind says, "Winter is coming!"
"Oh, the end of me!"
Or maybe it's—"I'm losing my mind!"
"Oh, love me, love me!"
And in the twilight my mezzanine
chills to the bone.

The dialogue 's incomprehensible
when you're alone.

Joseph Brodsky

Notes

"Deor" is preserved in the Exeter Book, an anthology of Anglo-Saxon poetry that was donated to the Exeter cathedral, where it still is, in 1071, by Leofric, the first bishop of Exeter. The poem is probably the work of a scop of the 9th century. It ends with a verse paragraph of Christian consolation which, feeling it to be at odds with the spirit of the poem, and disliking it, I have omitted. In Seamus Heaney's translation, published in *The Word Exchange: Anglo-Saxon Poems in Translation* (2010), the lines are retained.

"Venetian Prose": In January, 1954, following the report of Hemingway's death in a plane crash in Africa, Montale wrote an obituary for *Il Corriere della Serra*, the Milan newspaper he worked for. In March, he interviewed Hemingway in a hotel room in Venice. The obituary can be found online.

"Singing": cf. Siegfried Sassoon, "Everyone Sang." (Primo Levi's note)

"Sunset at Fossoli": cf. Catullus, *Catulli liber* 5,4. At Fossoli, near Modena, there was a detention and selection camp for prisoners destined for deportation. (Primo Levi's note)

Lines 6-9 are Walter Ralegh's translation of Catullus' lines.

"Pliny": By getting too close to the volcano, Pliny the Elder died in 79 A.D. during the eruption of Vesuvius that destroyed Pompeii. (Primo Levi's note)

The "nephew" in line 6 is Pliny the Younger, who described his uncle's final hours in a famous letter to Tacitus.

"Brown Battalion": cf. *Purgatorio*, Canto XXVI, l. 34. (Primo Levi's note)

"At Galvani's": Luigi Galvani (1737-1798) was an Italian doctor, anatomist, and professor at the University of Bologna, who discovered animal electricity. Legend has it that Galvani was skinning a frog at a table when his assistant (Primo Levi's hard-pressed and dismayed servant) touched an exposed nerve with a metal scalpel that picked up a charge.

Abbot Spallanzani is Lazaro Spallanzani (1729-1799), an Italian priest and biologist, who, according to the *Encyclopedia Britannica*, "studied the circulation of the blood, respiration, digestion, the senses of bats, the electricity of the torpedo, the breeding of eels and the regeneration of different appendages of Amphibia [Primo Levi's servant puts it less professorially], following the muscles, nerves and bones with a microscope. By filtering the semen he proved that spermatozoa were necessary for fertilization in different animals. He artificially inseminated a bitch."

"The Elephant": The blind hero is Hannibal, who, according to tradition, contracted an eye disease while crossing the Alps. (Primo Levi's note)

"Old Mole": cf. *Hamlet*, Act 1, Scene 5: 'old mole' (Primo Levi's note)

"The wind abandoned the woods": This poem and "For Schoolchildren," "I held those shoulders in my arms, and glanced," and "What do the bushes say to the wind" were all written between 1962 and 1964, when Joseph Brodsky was in his early twenties. They appear in *New Stanzas for Augusta: Poems to M. B.*, published by Ardis in 1983. M. B. are the initials of the woman Brodsky loved in Leningrad, and who bore his son. The book's title is an allusion to Byron's two poems entitled "Stanzas for Augusta."

"Odysseus to Telemachus": Brodsky left behind the young son when he was exiled from the Soviet Union in 1972.